Rug Weaving for Beginners

Small M's and O's rug, part of a 15-yard length woven by the author for the altar steps of a church, the yarns blended to match the marble. Weft distortion occurs, but does not affect the rug in use. Warp set at 4 e.p.i.

Rug Weaving for Beginners

By Margaret Seagroatt

Watson-Guptill Publications, New York

For Michael

Cover illustration Small wool rug from Yugoslavia. Wool warp set at 12 e.p.i. in tapestry technique, using slits and built-up shapes

First Printing, 1972

First published in the United States of America *1972* by Watson-Guptill Publications, a division of Billboard Publications, Inc., 165 West 46 Street, New York, N.Y.

Copyright © 1971 by Margaret Seagroatt
First published in Great Britain by Studio Vista Limited in 1971
General editors Brenda Herbert and Janey O'Riordan

Manufactured in the U.S.A.

Library of Congress Cataloging in Publication Data

Seagroatt, Margaret.
   Rug weaving for beginners.
   Bibliography: p.
     1. Hand weaving.   2. Rugs.   I. Title.
TT848.S39   1972   746.7   73-190517
ISBN 0-8230-4616-8

Contents

Acknowledgements

I would like to thank Frank McGonigal for the photographs; also students past and present at the Laird School of Art, Birkenhead, and Kirkby Fields College of Education (in particular Doreen Lancashire for the loan of her rugs in figs 53 and 82, Alison Denton-Griffin for the loan of her rug in fig. 100 and Nicholetta Sinclair for reading the manuscript);
also Harris Looms for the photograph in fig. 7;
Mrs P. Porter for the photograph of her rug in fig. 118;
The late Elaine Tankard for the gift of her rugs and design in figs 41, 58, 116, 117 and 124;
My husband for checking the text and proofs;
Peter Collingwood, whose teaching and writing have been a continuing inspiration.

Introduction

In an age of automation and increasing technological invention, the craft of rug weaving by hand might appear to be an anachronism. In spite of this, the interest in handweaving is increasing. There is a growing band of designer-weavers operating in their own studios; as well as a steady number of students, both amateur and professional, who are learning to practise the craft. What, then, is its justification in our modern world?

There is no point in weaving a rug by hand if a machine does it as well, or better. There is a vast industry concerned with the making of rugs; these rugs are produced in quantity, and are repeatable according to demand in a variety of colours and qualities. The handmade rug is different, and is not competing with the machine. It is usually a one-off piece, perhaps made to an individual requirement, and to a certain size. It takes longer to make, and because of this there are considerations other than the economics of the job. Yarns may be of high quality, perhaps specially spun or dyed: the colour may be so uniquely used that the rug is not exactly repeatable, and indeed may be so arranged that the colours are still being decided upon up to the last inch of weaving. A handwoven rug is the expression of the weaver's own personality in his choice of materials and the way he uses them. There is no need, even, for highly complex equipment, for very satisfactory rugs may be made on the simplest frame.

The aim of this book is to equip the beginner with a variety of techniques on simple equipment, which may lead to more complex efforts at a later stage. I have tried to keep the beginner's problems in mind, and to frame the answers to his questions in simple, non-technical language. Most of the illustrations, therefore, are of work by beginners, students and by the author as a student.

Design and colour

Design

A rug has basic requirements which should be taken into account when planning the design. It should be hard-wearing, warm, and should lie flat on the ground. The dyes used, whether the yarns are dyed at home or bought already dyed, should be fast to light. All these requirements are incorporated in the designing, which should spring from the technique to be used. A rug is a dominant element in a room, viewed from varying angles and distances, so that the design must be continuously interesting, both in its immediate impact and in its detail.

Before starting to design, beginners should make a sampler of several of the simpler techniques (see pp. 76, 79), so that these may be practised before using them in a large rug. This is important, otherwise the first effort may show a considerable difference in achievement between the beginning and the end. When weaving samples, look at the weave from a distance as well as on the loom; the scale of the weave alters substantially, and weaves which appear large close to may disappear totally at a distance. Simplicity is essential for first attempts, and it is better to limit the colour scheme to two or three colours until these can be controlled with certainty. First experiments with weave might very well use simple horizontal stripes as a motif, using differences in width and colour as the design element.

There are two main types of design—weave designs and free designs. Weave designs are controlled by the weaves used, and may be simple, as in some of the plain weave techniques, or complex, using the weave as a design element, as in all the examples using drafts, see pp. 45–57 and 80–91.

The technique having been chosen, the design may now be planned. Do a number of small designs until a satisfactory one evolves. This is a matter of trial and error, and these designs can be very rough sketches. When one is eventually chosen, a scale design should be made. If a free design is being used, as in a rya or tapestry rug, a half-scale plan on squared paper will be the most satisfactory. Dressmaker's $\frac{1}{4}''$ squared pattern paper, over-ruled in inches, is the best size for this purpose, and is cheaper than graph paper.

Colour

Beginners seem to have difficulty in using colour effectively, yet it is probably the most individual aspect of designing. People tend to be inhibited when using colour, yet have strong reactions to it. There are complex technical aspects, it is true, but it is possible to work in such a way that the beginner can build up confidence in his own powers of selection. Everyone has an individual reaction to colour, and everyday visual experiences may be used to stimulate and control it. Look closely at grass and you will find that it is made up of many different shades of green: a newly-dug garden, a window box or a ploughed field is not just a plain brown; flowers against these backgrounds emerge as isolated spots or masses of colour. Trees and buildings make dramatic impact against the sky, while a closer look at individual leaves or flowers reveal many shades.

Look at paintings, either originals or reproductions, and observe the colour combinations and proportions. Whether medieval or modern, unexpected juxtapositions are revealed, and a subtle blend of colours makes up a mass of colour. Magazines are readily available, as are advertisements, posters and woven fabrics. Keep notebooks of source material, noting, perhaps, the reasons for its appeal. Gradually a pattern will emerge, and with it a more positive guide to your own taste.

Colour proportion may be worked out by a simple method which works for most purposes. The colours of the rainbow are made up of the visible light rays, which appear in the order red, orange, yellow, green, blue and violet, red having the longest wave length, violet the shortest. When daylight, which is composed of these rays, shines on an object the colour rays of that object are reflected back to the eye, the others being absorbed. All the rays are reflected back from a white object, none from a black. Using this information, a colour

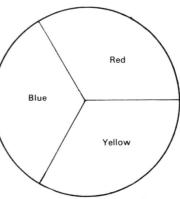

Fig 1   Primary colours

circle may be constructed. All colours are a mixture of the three primaries, red, yellow and blue (fig. 1), the eye only being sensitive to these three. Six secondary colours are made from a mixture of these (fig. 2); and a circle containing twelve colours may be made by a third mixture of the six colours (fig. 3). The colours follow their rainbow order, cold colours (tending towards blue) appearing opposite warm ones (tending towards red). Any three adjacent colours used together create a harmony. The colour which is opposite the middle one of the three on the colour circle is its complementary, and will be at its maximum intensity used in a small quantity with mixtures of the other three colours.

Practise colour blending by using three or four strands of carpet yarn together. By adding and dropping the different shades, make samples which gradually change from one colour to another. Then practise controlled blending of colours within the same range, using small quantities of the complementary colour as a contrasting motif. Experience will give confidence in the selection of colours, and the resulting rug will be unique to you. Examples of colour blending are shown in figs 82 and 100.

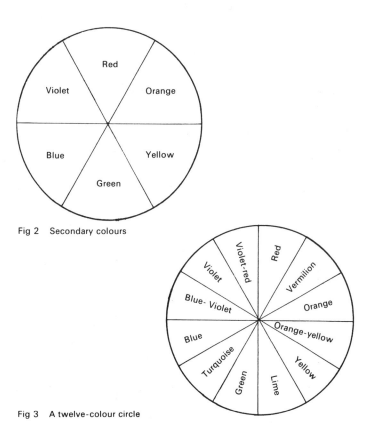

Fig 2   Secondary colours

Fig 3   A twelve-colour circle

Choice of loom

The choice of loom on which to make rugs is of first importance, as the size and type of rug to be made is dependent on the nature of the equipment. Large floor looms take up a great deal of space, as to a lesser extent do table looms. Bearing in mind that the most beautiful oriental carpets are often made on very primitive equipment, a simple frame loom may very well be the answer to the problems of space and money.

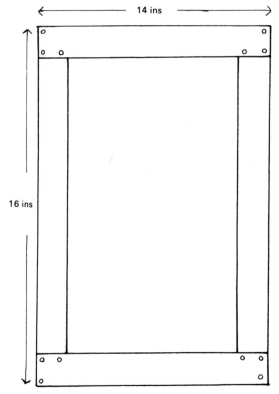

Fig 4   Frame loom

Frame looms

A simple frame may be made from 2 in. by 1 or ³/₄-in. batten, thin wood strip (fig. 4).
Materials needed
2 pieces of batten 16 ins long.
3 pieces of batten 14 ins long.
2 lengths of ¹/₂-in. dowel rod 14 ins long.
12 screws long enough to penetrate a double depth of batten.
4 cup hooks large enough to take the dowel rod.
21 2-in. nails.
2 thin ¹/₂-in. lathes 14 ins long.

Screw two of the 14-in. battens to the 16-in. lengths to form a rectangle. The screws should be countersunk for a neat finish, and the short sides should be uppermost so that the long sides form a support for the two ends. The screws go into the lower inside and two outside corners, the cup hook going into the top inside corner to give the maximum length of warp (the yarn stretched onto the frame or loom to form the basis of the weave). The hooks face outwards from the frame and should be bent far enough back for the dowel rods to rest in them (fig. 5). These are now the warp rods to which the warp is to be tied.

The reed or spacer (fig. 6), which keeps the warp accurately spaced, is made from the other piece of batten, the nails being knocked into the wood in a straight line, ¹/₂ in. apart. This gives a 10-in. reed to fit the weaving space in the centre of the frame, with a space, or dent, of ¹/₂ in.

The frame is now ready for a warp to be tied on. It is rigid and strong enough to withstand quite a strain, and will produce a sample of approximately 10 ins square.

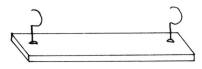

Fig 5   Cup hooks

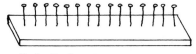

Fig 6   Reed or spacer

LARGER FRAMES

These may be made in a similar manner, and to any dimension required. Wider ones, however, may need more than two cup hooks, so that the rod does not sag in the centre when the warp is pulled tightly.

Improvized frames may be made from picture frames, bedsteads, large boxes etc., and if the corners are strengthened, either by screwing blocks of wood into them or using angle brackets, rugs of good quality can be made on them. An old deck chair is almost a ready-made frame. If a piece of string is tied between

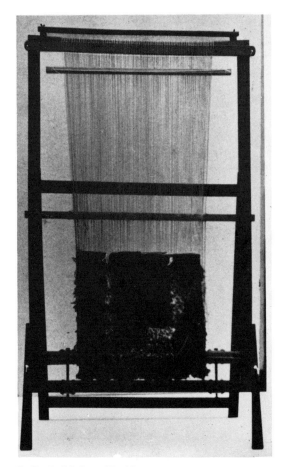

Fig 7   Upright loom (Harris)

the main frame and the pivoted leg, the frame will stand by itself, and fold when not in use. A frame has certain advantages over a loom where space is a consideration, as it may be stood against a wall when not being used.

Frames for rugmaking may be purchased (fig. 7), and though the instructions may differ slightly from the ones I have given, the principle remains the same. Some may recommend winding the warp onto the frame as a continuous thread (see p. 27). If it is tied to two rods, however, the tension may be altered on individual threads where necessary, as on a loom. On a very large frame, where the rods have to be thicker to take the increased strain, they are better tied to the frame direct, and broom handles may be used. This will, in any case, be necessary where a metal frame like a bedstead is used, and has the added advantage that the length of the warp may be exactly adjusted. If the rods are attached by slip knots this can be done quite easily (fig. 8).

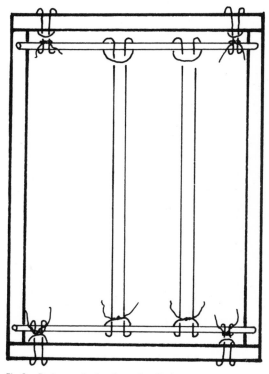

Fig 8   Rods attached to frame by slip knots

The loom

A loom is really an extension of the frame, and if it is thought of in this way no confusion should arise. There are several types of loom suitable for rugs, mainly table looms, floor looms and upright looms. The upright types are called high-warp looms, the others low-warp.

TABLE LOOM

A table loom (fig. 9) is not usually strong enough for making rugs, as a rug must be heavily beaten. A 24-in. wide rug may be made reasonably satisfactorily, but anything wider is better made on one of the other looms. The main advantage of a table loom is that it is small and light enough to move about, and may be stood on a suitable table and put away when out of use.

The basic framework of a table loom is built on rather similar principles to the frame loom. Two rollers have been added and the whole warp is made, and attached to the back roller by means of a rod. The warp is then wound onto the back roller, the threads passed through the lifting and spacing mechanism, and tied on to the front roller by means of another rod. The reed is enclosed in a frame, or batten, which beats the weft (the yarn which passes under and over the warp threads).

The woven rug may then be wound onto the front roller, and

Fig 9   Table loom (Harris)

the weaving is quicker than on the frame. As this loom has four shafts, which each control one set of threads, a greater range of patterns may be woven than on a frame.

FLOOR LOOM

This is a further extension of the table loom. It stands on the floor, as its name implies, and the lifting mechanism is controlled by pedals, which usually lift two shafts at a time (fig. 10). The best type of floor loom is a sturdy four-poster with an overhead beater. This gives the maximum strength and rigidity, and the beating of the weft is made easier by the swinging batten.

Fig 10   Floor loom (Harris)

UPRIGHT LOOM

This loom usually has only two shafts, so that pattern weaving is limited, but has the advantage that it takes up very little floor space. Similar to the frame made from a deck chair, the warp runs vertically instead of horizontally. This means that the beating of the rug is always in a downward direction, which is easier to operate. It also has the advantage that the whole rug is visible while the weaving is progressing (fig. 11).

The emphasis on the strength and rigidity of a loom is because for rug weaving the warp is usually of an unresilient material such as linen or hemp, and the tension must be extremely tight in order to beat the weft enough to cover it. This imposes an enormous strain on the framework, which could make it fall to pieces. Rollers, too, must be strong enough to withstand the strain. So buy the largest and strongest loom that money and space allow.

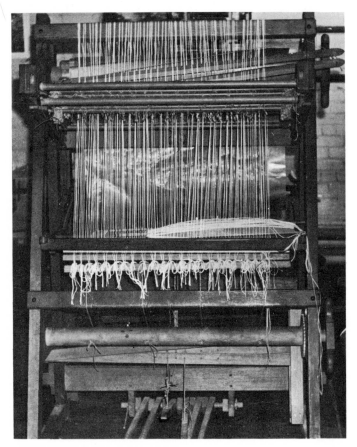

Fig 11   Upright loom with beater (Harris)

Miscellaneous equipment

Beater

Any work on a frame will require some sort of portable beater to beat down the weft (fig. 12). This may be of metal, or wood weighted with lead, and ideally is used with an upright loom or frame, as the force of gravity works with the weight of the beater.

A beater may be improvized from a heavy table fork (fig. 13), the leverage from holding the fork at its extreme end compensating for its lighter weight. A beater may be used with a horizontal loom if the action of the batten is not strong enough, as with some table looms.

Reed hook

A flat piece of metal, notched at either end to draw the warp through the reed. The notches should be big enough to take a doubled end of rug warp (fig. 14).

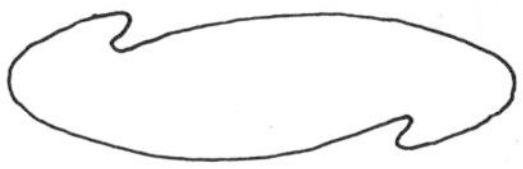

Threading hook

This also applies to the thread-ing hook, which should be large

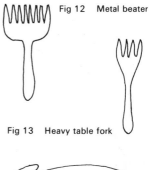

Fig 12   Metal beater

Fig 13   Heavy table fork

Fig 14   Reed hook

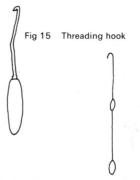

Fig 15   Threading hook

Fig 16   Threading hook made from wire heald

enough to take the warp, but small enough to go through the heald (see p. 36) with it (fig. 15). Most threading hooks are too small for this purpose, but a special rug hook has been designed (see p. 102). An improvized hook may be made from a wire heald, cut off at one end and bent over, but this does not last long (fig. 16). An old-fashioned button hook might do for large healds, especially string ones.

Raddle

A spacing device, or raddle, is needed for spacing out the warp to the correct width before winding it onto the back roller. This may be either of wood with $1/2$-in. spaces (fig. 17) or metal with $1/4$-in. spaces, or improvized from a piece of wood with nails. The principle is the same: a piece of wood as long as the width of the rug is set with pegs or metal teeth. Usually a cap is provided to stop the warp slipping out, but I prefer to wind a long piece of string round the pegs for extra security.

A good improvization may be made with a piece of 2-in. by $3/4$-in. batten, or wood of similar size, set with rustless nails at $1/2$-in. intervals. To prevent the wood splitting, stagger the setting in two rows. These are so cheap and easy to make that you can have two or three in different widths. Otherwise buy one as wide, or a little wider than your loom, and space smaller warps in the middle.

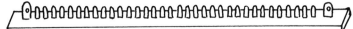

Fig 17   Raddle

Shuttles

A shuttle is an important tool, and it may be one of three types:
1. An ordinary stick shuttle, notched at both ends on which the weft is wound from end to end (fig. 18). This, although it is sold in sizes made for rug weaving, is not the most suitable type, as the notches tend to catch in the warp and pull it, to the detriment of the tension.
2. The ski shuttle (fig. 19) weaves flat through the shed or weaving space and is only $1 1/4$ ins high, so it is the best to use on a horizontal loom, especially if there is a narrow shed. It is 24 ins long, with the weft wound round the hooks, but is easily thrown from side to side, so it has several advantages.
3. The netting-type shuttle (fig. 20) also has advantages over the stick shuttle. It is 32 ins long, and the weft is wound round the notched end and over the spike in the middle on alternate sides. It takes roughly $1/4$lb. of yarn, but is fairly bulky when full, and

difficult to push through a narrow shed or weaving space. I solved this problem by having some made to the same design but longer, so that the tip reached the edges of the warp and could be pulled through. The weft was also not so bulky when wound. This shuttle may be obtained in an 11-in. size, suitable for rug samples.

A number of shuttles is always needed, either for winding different colours, or simply to speed up the weaving by having several available.

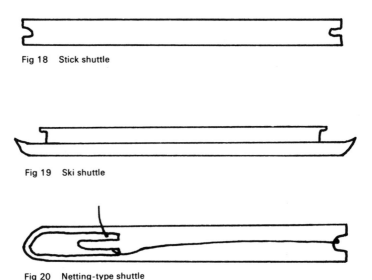

Fig 18   Stick shuttle

Fig 19   Ski shuttle

Fig 20   Netting-type shuttle

Temple or tenterhook

This is a device for holding the weaving at its specified width, so that it may be kept even (fig. 21). It is made of two pieces of flat wood, with metal teeth at either end. The pieces slide into one another, and are adjustable. The teeth are inserted into the selvedge at both edges and the temple is adjusted until it is the right width. The temple should be moved up every inch or two, so that the newest weaving is always close to it.

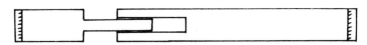

Fig 21   Temple or tenterhook

Winders

These may be of several types. The ordinary wire wool winder is reasonably adequate, but not really big enough to take a large quantity of rug wool. The Swedish umbrella type of winder is very suitable, especially if it is fixed horizontally instead of vertically (fig. 22). There is also an industrial horizontal winder. Several winders may be needed when blending yarns together.

It is more time-consuming, but yarns may be wound into balls for blending. The balls are put into separate containers and wound onto the shuttle.

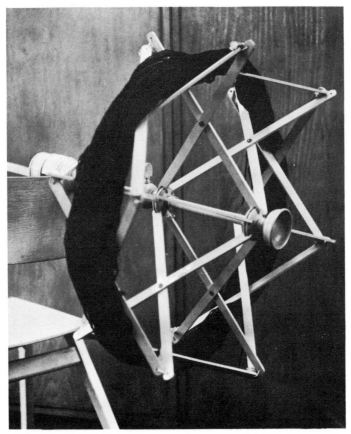

Fig 22   Swedish umbrella skeiner

Warp

The yarn stretched onto the frame or loom to form the basis of the weave is called the warp. This is a fixed factor, i.e. it cannot be changed once weaving begins. A rug warp must be strong, and may be of cotton, linen, ramie, hemp or jute (see below). It must be smooth, so that the weft is easily beaten down over it, but not so smooth that it slips about. It must be tightly spun, so that its strength is increased. The strength of finer yarns may always be increased by doubling or trebling them.

Cotton

The easiest yarn to use, cotton is both strong and resilient. It knots easily for fringing, and usually comes in off-white shades, though some of the excellent, tightly-twisted twines used in the fishing industry for net-making come in shades of brown.

A sub-tropical shrub, cotton fibres vary in length from between $1/_2$ and $2^1/_2$ ins, being tightly twisted to make a strong yarn.

Linen or flax

Linen is a strong but inelastic yarn, and a linen warp gives a rug a firm quality. It may be bleached, but in its natural state comes in shades varying from pale straw to dark grey. Its long fibres, between 2 and 3 feet, grow between the bark and the inner core of the plant, and have to be steeped in water to separate them.

Ramie

Ramie grows mainly in warmer climates. Its fibre is longer and not so smooth, but its properties and uses are similar to linen.

Hemp

Again, the fibre is similar to linen, but coarser and stiffer, its fibres growing to 6 feet long. It is widely used for rug warp.

Jute

The longest, coarsest and weakest stem fibre, it is still strong enough for a warp yarn, having similar properties to hemp and linen.

Most of these yarns dye well with cotton dyes, though linen may have to be steeped in the dyebath overnight, and the natural colours of the yarns affect the finished result.

Tension and strain

The main hazard to which a warp is subjected is that of strain, which is related to the tension. The warp for a rug must be stretched as tightly as possible to enable the weft to be beaten down more closely, and this not only imposes a strain on the loom, but on the warp itself. The yarn chosen for the warp must, therefore, be the strongest possible compatible with its use. As the weft in a wool rug must cover the warp, it must be as rigid as possible, so that a linen, hemp, ramie or jute yarn would be suitable, being in varying degrees smooth, stiff and strong. Certain synthetics may also be used, but the novice should be wary of these, since some of them tend to stretch, or to fluff and break away in the weaving.

If, however, the warp is to show, as in mattings made of stiff materials such as rush, an unresilient yarn is not suitable, as the warp has to bend round the weft (fig. 23). The extra yarn needed for this is called the take-up, and allowance has to be made for it. Cotton is the best yarn here, being resilient, but strong enough to take the wear. It also beds down slightly on the weft, so is more resistant to rubbing.

Calculating the warp

Before starting to calculate the amount of yarn needed, the width of the rug and the number of threads or ends per inch (e.p.i.) must be known. This will vary according to the type of rug. A wool rug may have a setting of between 3 and 8 e.p.i., depending on the size of the weft and the technique. Mattings may use between

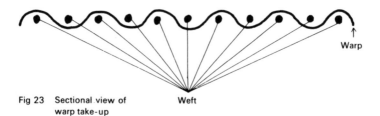

Fig 23   Sectional view of   Weft
         warp take-up

3 and 5 e.p.i. A warp-face rug, on the other hand, may be set as closely as 12 e.p.i. The captions to the rugs illustrated describe the warp settings, which will give you some idea of possible setting for the various techniques.

The length of the finished rug must be known, and this is added to the length of the wastage, which includes the fringe (with allowance for knots) and the unwoven warp left after weaving. For weft-face rugs this should be approximately 27 ins, but on a frame this may be less, as there will not be so much warp left after weaving. Mattings may require a take-up of a yard to a yard and a half if the weft is very thick. The calculation is expressed in simple steps in the following example:

Width of warp	30 ins	Length of warp	50 ins
Ends per inch	4	Wastage	27 ins
Number of ends	30 × 4 120	Total length	77 ins
Selvedge	2	Ends × total length	261 yds
Total number of ends	122		approximately

Using a thick warp of about 660 yards per pound the warp for this rug would take about 7 oz. The average amount needed varies between $\frac{1}{4}$lb and 1lb according to the size of the rug and the thickness of the yarn.

The selvedge

The extra thread needed to strengthen and thicken each edge is called the selvedge (fig. 24). This is placed in with the last one or two ends, and will therefore not affect the calculation of the width. The selvedge should be set closer at the edge if the count of the reed allows this, and if the rug is wide an extra two ends at each edge will be necessary.

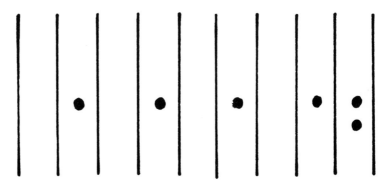

Fig 24   Selvedge: sectional view of warp ends

Warping on the frame

This is a suitable method for use on small frames. The alternative method may be easier for larger frames.

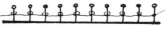

Fig 25   Winding thread round nails

Spacing the warp

Place the raddle across the frame. This has $1/2$-in. spaces, so that if the setting is 4 e.p.i. two working ends will have to be placed in each space. As work proceeds, wind a thread round the nails to keep the warp in place (fig. 25).

Measuring and tying the warp

Measure the length of the frame plus about 9 ins and cut the warp double this length. This gives either two single working ends or one double one. The loop formed by the doubled warp is placed over

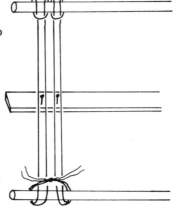

Fig 26   Tying a group of ends

the warp rod, brought back underneath, and the long end pulled through. This gives a firm loop to pull against when tying the other end. Go on doing this until sufficient warp ends are attached to the rod, including the selvedge.

Taking groups of ends occupying not more than an inch of raddle space, place them over the front rod and divide them in half. The two halves then go under the rod and a reef knot is tied over the ends (fig. 26).

Tension

The tension is important, and in each group warps must be tied on at an even tension. This should be taut, but not so taut that the rods will break or a shed cannot be raised.

An alternative method

Another method of attaching a warp to a frame is to pass it continuously round the rods and through the raddle in a figure of eight, keeping the tension taut (fig. 27). When it is completely wound, and both ends tied securely to the warp rod, the over-all tension may be adjusted by tightening the ties of the warp rod. This is a more suitable method for a large frame. The commercial frames may be different in detail, but they operate on the same principle.

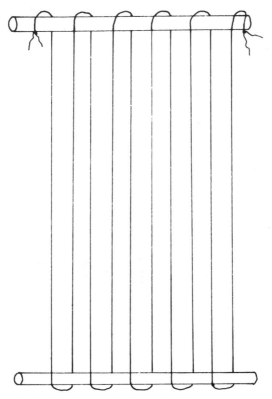

Fig 27   Winding warp in a figure-of-eight

Longer warps

A warp longer than the length of the frame may be made by carry-ing the warp right round the frame, and attaching it to a third warp rod (fig. 28). This warp rod is attached to the front one with the usual slip loops and knots, and the weaving may be moved round the frame by removing the back rod to loosen the tension, and then inserting a fourth rod in place of the first, which has moved round with the weaving (fig. 29).

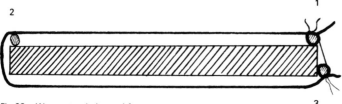

Fig 28   Warp extended round frame

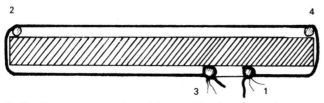

Fig 29   Woven warp moved round frame and fourth rod inserted

Preparing a warp for the loom

A rug woven on a frame is completely visible from start to finish. This is not the case with a loom, as only the part which is being woven can be seen, and the unwoven warp has to be rolled onto the back roller of a loom, being gradually unrolled as the finished work is rolled onto the front roller. This is achieved by means of a warping frame.

The warping frame

A good warping frame may be made from an old picture frame strengthened at the corners. The frame should be strong enough to have holes bored to take removable pegs, $\frac{5}{8}$-in. dowel rod being a useful size for these. The holes may be bored as in fig. 30. A warping board may be made to a similar plan, using strong wood for the base. On the other hand I have known a weaver who improvized a warping board from large nails banged into the bathroom door!

The main requirements are three pegs at one end and two at the other, the ones in between being distributed to allow different lengths of warp to be made. It is quite a good plan to make the frame in a width which is easily calculated, such as 36 ins.

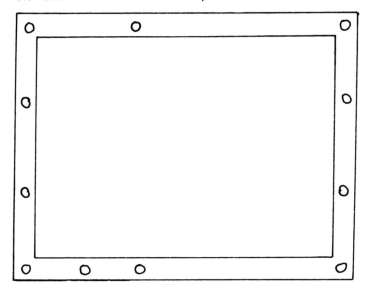

Fig 30　Warping frame

Warping

Start at the end with two pegs, and make a large loop in the warp. Place this over the first peg, then pass it under the second, and round as many pegs as are needed until the other end is reached. It is not necessary to have all the pegs in if only a short warp is needed. When the last three pegs are reached wind under and over, round the last peg, and then wind back again over and under, so that the threads cross each other, then back again to the first peg (fig. 31). These are the crosses, and there should be two at one end, and one at the other. Continue winding until the required number of threads has been wound, using an extra thread to count them in groups, which may be conveniently related to the warp setting, i.e. groups of eight if the warp is set at 4 e.p.i., so that the counting is done in 2-in. sections (fig. 32). When the end of the warp is reached a loop is tied again and slipped over the peg. The warp is now ready to tie.

Tying the crosses

It is very important not to lose the cross, because this is what keeps the order of the threads. A rug warp is usually composed

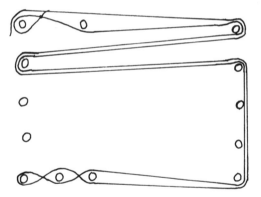

Fig 31   Winding the warp

Fig 32   Counting thread

of coarse yarns which tend to slip about, and the method of tying indicated minimises this, and makes the cross very easy to separate. The warp is tied at both sides of each cross (fig. 33). Six ties are needed at one end, four at the other. This may seem a little unnecessary, but the results justify the few minutes extra trouble, and mistakes are avoided. The ties should be bows so that they are firm but easily pulled undone. Do *not* cut with scissors lest the warp should accidentally be cut.

Chaining

A rug warp is usually fairly short, but if more than one rug is to be made a longer warp will be needed. As this will be unwieldy to manage when winding it onto the roller, the warp is chained. Push the hand through the loop at the end with one cross (this should be made larger than the others), grasp the warp and pull it through, making a loop (fig. 34). Do the same with this loop, until 18 ins of warp is left. This is really a large scale crochet chain, using the hand as a crochet hook. Push a stick through the end loop to hold it, taking it out when the chain is to be undone.

Fig 33   Tying the cross

Fig 34   Chaining the warp

Warping on the loom

Having made the warp and ensured that the threads are in order from end to end, it must now be attached to the loom. As the warp is longer than the loom is deep, the part which is not immediately being worked on is wound round the back roller. In order to do this the warp has first to be spaced, the raddle being used for this purpose.

Raddling

It is easier to raddle on a table than on the loom. Take the back stick from the loom, and push it through the end loop of the warp. Firmly attach a long piece of strong yarn to one end of the stick, and draw this through the other side of the cross, tying it firmly to the other end of the stick. This has two purposes, to keep the warps in order and to hold the loops close against the back stick to minimise their movement. It also helps to clear the shed when the last few inches of rug are woven. Holes may be drilled at either end of the stick to keep the ties firm (fig. 35A).

In each side of the second cross place two shed sticks, tying them parallel with a figure-of-eight tie, which keeps the sticks lying flat (fig. 35B). Tie with a bow, because this is untied when the raddling is done. These sticks provide a second check on the order if the yarn round the first cross should break, and is easier to count from. Check that all the sticks are tied, then undo the ties round the crosses. Place the warp on the table with the shed sticks between you and the raddle, and the rest of the warp lying across it on the left. Working from right to left, and using the crossing point of the warp between the sticks as a guide, take the number of warps, in order, which occupy one space in the raddle, and place these in the space. Wind a piece of yarn round the pegs in the raddle as the work proceeds. I prefer this to the normal raddle cap, which is placed over the warp afterwards; because the yarn keeps the warp in place should the raddle tip over while working on it. To avoid this, clamp the raddle to the table, or support it by standing something heavy on either side. If the raddle is wider than the warp, make sure that the warp is centrally spaced. When the whole warp is spaced the shed sticks may be removed.

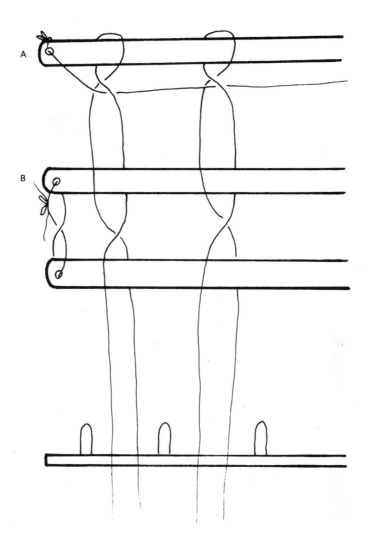

A

B

Fig 35   Raddling the warp

Attaching the warp

(1) Carry the raddled warp to the loom, and attach the stick to the loom with slip knots, using the raddle to divide the warp between the knots. Rest the raddle on the back bar of the loom and, passing the warp under the bar and back over the raddle towards you, tie the raddle onto the back bar. The warp may then be wound onto the back roller without moving to the front, and without disturbing the loom (fig. 36).

(2) Strong brown paper is required, a little wider than the warp. This is to stop the warp piling up unevenly, and enables it to be tightened between the layers. The warp is then wound round the back roller with the paper until an inch or so has been drawn in to secure it. (3) Making sure that the warp is evenly spread along the back stick, take the whole warp in the hand and pull tight, smoothing the threads with the fingers until the warp is at an even tension. Take care that the loops round the stick do not move about too much, or the warp will become uneven in length. Pull towards you steadily until completely taut, then relax the tension. This process is repeated until enough warp is wound. Pull quite steadily at right-angles to the roller, or the warp will be wound at an angle, and the tension will suffer. Leave enough warp to reach to the front of the loom.

(4) When this stage is reached, pull the yarn wound round the raddle, and release the warp, which should now be placed over the bar, towards the front of the loom. (5) The shed sticks are inserted into the single cross, and tied, edging them down the warp near the back bar. (6) Cut through the loops at the end of the warp, which should now be supported by two sticks resting at each side of the back and front bars, passing right through the loom.

An easy way

A quick way of warping, especially for narrow and short warps, is to make the warp in the usual way (p. 30), tying the cross to the back stick, and attaching it to the loom. A stick is passed through the loop at the other end, and the ends of the stick rested and caught between two chairs. The warp is spread out as evenly as possible, and a piece of board, or a reed is placed on the stick. These are held tightly together and the warp is wound round them, the weaver moving towards the loom until the wound warp is resting against it, keeping the tension quite taut. The warp may then be wound onto the loom, releasing it from the board while keeping it at tension. This may not be so accurate as the more conventional method, but with care, a warp may be wound on very quickly without a raddle.

Whichever way is chosen, the warping can be done by one person without assistance.

Fig 36   The raddled warp ready to be wound onto the loom

Threading

As in weaving on a frame, the warp has to be tied to the front of the loom, but before doing so, it has to pass through two devices which automatically produce a shed, space the warp and beat it down — the healds and the reed.

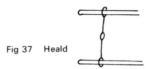

Fig 37   Heald

The healds

The warps are first passed individually through the healds, using a threading hook. A heald consists of a length of fine wire twisted into a loop in the middle and mounted on a frame (fig. 37). Healds may also be made of string. The shed sticks are placed close to the healds, and taking them in the order of the cross between the sticks, the threads are pulled one by one through a heald, in the sequence in which they are to be threaded. To facilitate this, small groups of healds may be separated from the main body as the threading proceeds, i.e. if the sequence 1, 2, 3, 4, is used, these four

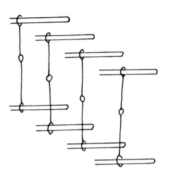

Fig 38   Four separated healds

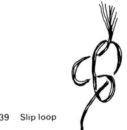

Fig 39   Slip loop

healds are separated from the rest and threaded (fig. 38). This lessens the possibility of mistakes. Check every group of eight threads to make sure that the threading is correct, and tie together in a slip loop (fig. 39) so that they may be easily undone.

The reed

The warp is now ready to be passed through the reed. This is the device which keeps the warp accurately spaced, and as it is mounted in a movable frame called a batten, or beater, it is also the means by which the weft is beaten down. Using the reed hook, the warp is passed in order through the spaces in the reed. To facilitate this, four threads are used at once, separating them with the fingers of the left hand (fig. 40). It is then an easy matter to select each thread for passing through the reed, tying and checking them in eights with a slip loop on the other side. The number of threads passed through the reed will depend on the number of spaces, or dents, to the inch. Rug warps are widely spaced by comparison with other types of warp. Reeds of various dentages may be purchased, an eight and a ten being convenient sizes. These are wide enough to take a thick warp, strong enough to beat down heavily, and also allow the selvedge to be threaded in adjacent dents. Threading through alternate dents gives four and five to the inch respectively, and an approximate three on both if two spaces are missed. Both, of course, may be threaded in multiples for finer warps, possible settings being sixteen, twenty, twenty-four etc. on the eight's reed, and twenty, twenty-five and thirty on the ten's. Reeds are also available in three, four, five and six settings.

Tying on

The warp is tied to the stick attached to the front roller in the same way as on the frame loom, tying in convenient groups of not more than an inch, keeping a taut and even tension. Check the tension by tightening the roller, and retie any ends which are slack.

The warp is now ready to be woven.

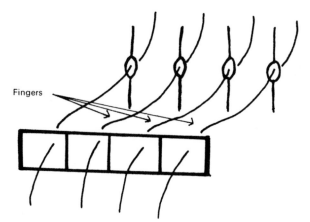

Fingers

Fig 40   Separating with the fingers

Weft

The yarns which pass over and under the warp between each edge are called the weft. These must be strong enough to withstand heavy wear, and must pack down closely.

Wool

The most usual weft for a rug is wool, which comes from the sheep (fig. 41), and preferably from a breed which has a coarse fleece. Wool fibre has a unique construction, being covered with horny scales which overlap one another like roof tiles. This makes it elastic, resilient, warm and capable of being dyed easily. There are many sheep breeds from which woollen yarns are spun, all with varying characteristics, so that it is essential to buy a yarn which has been specially spun for the purpose. Knitting yarns will *not* do, as they are too soft, and do not wear well. The most usual yarn available is the two-ply carpet yarn spun for industry.

This comes in varying thicknesses, according to the manufacturer, and three or four are wound together on a shuttle, and used as a single yarn. This ensures a greater flexibility in colour, and makes the weft softer, and more easily beaten down. If a harder effect is wanted, a six-ply rug yarn, which is the equivalent of three or four strands of two-ply, may be used. Wool may also be used as weft in its unspun state (see p. 56).

It is sometimes possible to buy industrial waste yarns, which may be tangled skeins or the unused ends from carpet manufacture. These are sometimes in a continuous length, or in the form of short or long thrums (the unused warp ends from carpet weaving). Short thrums are really short, and only suitable for knotting, but long thrums are long enough to use for weft. It is not usually possible to specify exact requirements, as supplies depend on what the mills have discarded, though firms are usually able to supply mixtures of similar colours. This yarn is much cheaper than buying in the usual way.

Other yarns

Hair yarns, such as mohair, goat, camel, horse and cow, may be used as weft. Their characteristics are somewhat similar to wool, and yarns suitable for rugs are spun from the coarser, longer part of the animal's coat. It is wise to experiment with these before

Fig 41 A close-pile wool rug, woven on a frame. The pile is a single strand of six-ply, with ½-in. Ghiordes knot, separated by two picks of six-ply set at 4 e.p.i. The weaver's second rug, this design follows the same type of striped pattern as her first (fig 58). A macramé fringe finishes the ends

use, as they are much springier than wool and do not beat down so well, so that the warp setting or the amount of weft may have to be adjusted.

Wool weft is mainly used to cover the warp. There are other yarns, used for mattings, which allow the warp to show. These are mostly made from hard, unresilient vegetable fibres, which lie across the warp without bending. Most of these absorb water without harm, so are suitable for bathroom and kitchen use. They include cane, coir, rush, seagrass, sisal, unspun jute and hemp,

Fig 42 Matting sample, with cotton warp set at 3 e.p.i. Jute, ramie and raffia weft, ends finished with divided knots

woven in conjunction with any of the warp yarns used as weft (figs 42 and 43). Various synthetics may also be used, and experiment in this field is recommended.

Watch the tension when weaving with any of these rigid materials. If the thick material is always used on the same shed, i.e. with the same warp threads raised, the take-up on that shed, is greater, and these warps will tighten, the others growing looser. It is desirable to devise a weaving sequence which will bring thick and thin picks (rows of weft) regularly on both sheds.

Calculating the weft

There is no fixed formula for calculating rug weft, as much will depend on the setting, the technique and the closeness of the beating. A very rough guide is that a square yard will use two pounds of yarn. When weaving a symmetrical design in several colours, make sure that the yarn is divided into equal quantities and enough left to finish the rug, as it may be impossible to match the colours exactly.

Fig 43   Mat with warp of red, white and black cotton twine, set at 3 e.p.i. Plaited rush and dyed red sisal weft

Weaving

The weft has first to be wound onto a shuttle, which should be of a size suitable to the width of the warp (see p. 20). This should be made as taut as possible before weaving begins. Two sticks are then inserted in alternate sheds to spread the warp to its proper spacing.

On the frame

There are two methods of obtaining a shed on a frame. The simplest way, for use on a small sample frame, is by using two sticks. Weave the first stick over and under alternate warps, then turn it up on its side. This makes the space, or shed, through which the weft is to pass. Pass the first pick of weft through this shed, and then push the stick to the other end of the frame, away from the weaving. Another stick is then woven through the opposite set of warps, using the first stick as a guide (fig. 44). This is then brought down to push the weaving into place. After the second pick the stick is withdrawn, and the first stick brought down again. This means that one stick stays in the warp all the time, while the other is darned in on alternate rows.

This is quite quick on a small sample, but a bigger frame needs a further refinement. Loops of strong yarn are passed round alternate warps, and tied into convenient groups (fig. 45). These

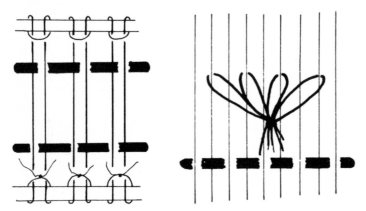

Fig 44   Sticks woven through opposite sheds

Fig 45   Loops to lift second shed

are pulled forward to make the second shed, a stick making the first shed as before.

The weft must be beaten down firmly and evenly with a beater or heavy table fork.

Selvedges

The selvedge not only has an extra thread in the warp, but has to have extra thickness in the weft to compensate for the bulk lost in a single turn round the selvedge. A firmer edge will result if two turns are taken round the end warp (fig. 46).

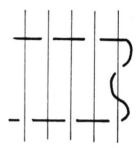

Fig 46   Extra bulk at selvedge

Single rows of alternating colours need a slightly different treatment to avoid an untidy selvedge. An uneven number of warps are required, otherwise the selvedges will be different. One colour goes right to each edge, making two turns round the end warp. The other colour turns just before the selvedge, passing under the first colour at the edge and being hidden by it. This makes a firm, neat edge (fig. 47).

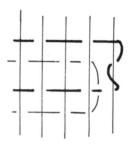

Fig 47   Pick-and-pick selvedge

Starting to weave

When the first pick of weaving is made, an end is left hanging out. This is spliced as in fig. 48, the aim being to keep the weft an even thickness throughout its length. Joins are made in the same way (fig. 49), the ends

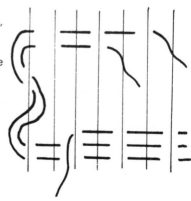

Fig 48   Splicing

being darned into the body of the rug parallel to the warp. It is very important to keep the weft loose, though not so loose that it forms bumps. On a frame this is achieved by beating down from the edge the weft is looped round, gradually working towards the shuttle, so that a little more yarn may be fed into the weaving as necessary. On a loom keep the yarn at an angle, 'bubbling' it at intervals to loosen it (fig. 50). If the shed, made by raising a pair of shafts, is changed before beating, the weft is held in place. Experiment will show how much to bubble it. Before starting another row the weft should be pulled tight at the selvedge to make sure it is firm. Experience will reveal how tightly it may be pulled without altering the width of the rug. The weft will inevitably pull the warp in slightly, but this should be kept to the minimum, or the rug will have uneven edges, the selvedge will wear against the reed and break, and worst of all, it will be impossible to beat down closely.

A heading of about one inch is usually woven at both ends of the rug, using the same material as the warp.

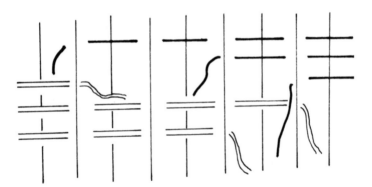

Fig 49   Spliced join

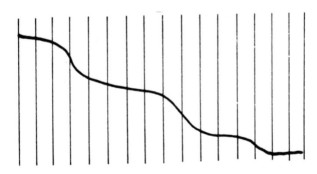

Fig 50   Bubbling weft at an angle

Plain weave

Plain weave, sometimes called tabby, is the simple interlacing of threads, in which the weft passes over and under alternate warp ends (fig. 51). The differences lie in the setting, the materials used, and in the use of various techniques.

The weft-face weave

The most common type of plain weave for rugs is weft-faced, i.e. the warp is totally covered by the weft. The warp must be set so that it is easily covered by the weft (fig. 52).

The most usual setting for this type of weave is approximately three or four e.p.i. when three or four strands of two-ply carpet rug yarn are used; five or six e.p.i. when a single strand of two-ply is used. The latter will give a thinner rug. Carpet yarns vary slightly in thickness according to the supplier, so that judgement must be exercised as to which thickness and setting is needed. A sample should be made if in doubt. When the setting is a wide one, i.e., three or four e.p.i., it is advisable to use two warp yarns working as one, as this makes the structure thicker and firmer.

Because the weft covers the warp completely, it presents a flat plane on which simple

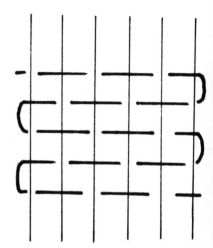

Fig 51   Plain weave

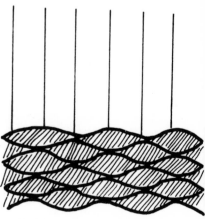

Fig 52   Weft covering warp

Fig 53   A student's first rug, on a cotton warp set at 3 e.p.i. The 1 ¹/₂-in. pile weft
is knotted at 1-in. intervals with three strands of two-ply in each Ghiordes knot.
The finely striped ground weave is broken by spots

designs are possible. The simplest of these uses horizontal stripes. These may be of varying widths, and in a combination of colours, and it is advisable to design them first on paper.

A combination of two picks of one colour and two picks of a contrasting colour will give a fine stripe, which undulates slightly. This is useful for a background weave to show up something stronger as in fig. 53, where a design of solid tufts in black and white contrasts with the finely-striped ground.

The use of three picks of each colour still gives a slightly uneven stripe (fig. 54), but four or more picks in each colour enables a more solid stripe to be built up (fig. 55).

Vertical stripes are produced by weaving alternate picks in contrasting colours, the width of the stripe being controlled by the setting (fig. 56). It will be seen that the dark colour always covers warps 1, 3, 5 etc., while the light colour covers warps 2, 4, 6 etc., so that alternating stripes of dark and light are produced when the weft is closely beaten. Note the special selvedge for pick-and-pick on page 43.

Vertical and horizontal stripes may be combined to make a toothed effect. Several rows of pick-and-pick produce a vertical stripe; using one of the colours of the stripe a block of solid colour is woven, the stripe merging into this. The first rows of pick-and-pick are then repeated, making sure that the stripes occur on the same warp ends as before (fig. 57).

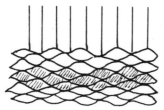

Fig 54   Three picks of each colour

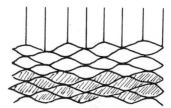

Fig 55   Four picks of each colour

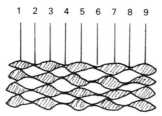

Fig 56   Vertical stripes

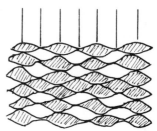

Fig 57   Toothed effect

Fig 58   A first rug, woven on a frame. The linen warp is set at 4 e.p.i., with six-ply weft. Knots cover the edges of the striped squares, which are woven with slits and sewn. The lattice design is knotted against a ground of broader stripes woven in four picks of each colour

With a little experience, the combinations of horizontal striping with bands of plain colour produce a satisfying rug. Fig. 58 shows a detail from a rug woven on a frame in these techniques, the shapes outlined in tufting.

So far we have dealt with techniques using colour contrasts. Colour blending may be used for more subtle effects, and for an extension of the colour graduations discussed on p. 11, using three or four two-ply yarns wound together on the shuttle (see frontispiece and fig. 100). Simple patterns may be produced by gradually blending shades into one another, either by throwing the weft from selvedge to selvedge, or by one of the tapestry techniques (see pp. 58–63).

A variation on this is to use one thread of light and three of dark wound together, contrasting with one dark and three light. The use of sharply-contrasting colours will produce a speckle (fig. 59), and the random winding, rather than a regular plying, produces the illusion of movement. These may be woven in

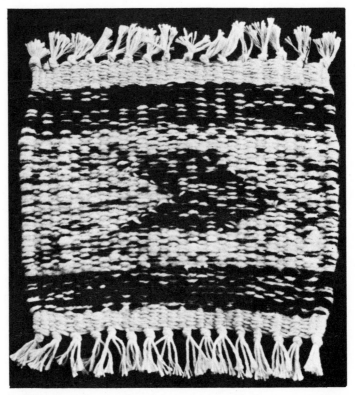

Fig 59   Rug sample using three dark, one light thread against a ground of three light, one dark

contrasting blocks, either as an arrangement of broad stripes (too narrow a stripe will not show up adequately), or in any of the tapestry techniques.

A more controlled version, using one shuttle, is to wind an equal quantity of dark and light yarns on to the shuttle. If woven in a random manner this will produce an all-over speckle, but the twist of the yarn may also be controlled by hand (fig. 60). If the dark yarn is to predominate, make it cover the light for a short distance by bringing it to the top with the fingers. The dark yarn will then appear on the front of the rug, the light being left at the back, making a more or less all black figure on one side, reversing to a white figure on the other side. Variations on this technique are possible, and patterns are produced quickly with only one shuttle.

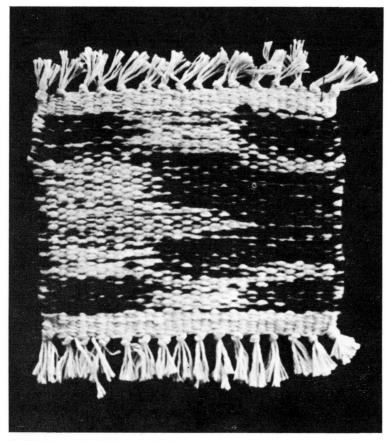

Fig 60   Rug sample, design controlled by twist

The warp-face weave

This is the exact opposite of the weft-face weave. Where the warp was widely spaced so that it could be covered by the weft, it is now very closely spaced, so that the weft does not show at all. This means that the warp yarn must be considered carefully. Most of the woollen yarns used for weft will be suitable, and in addition any hard-spun yarn—worsted, mohair belting yarn, etc.—will be easy to handle. Very soft, loosely spun rug yarn will not be so suitable, as it may not be strong enough to take the tension, and may in addition be too fluffy to let the warp move up and down without a struggle.

Fig 61   Warp-face sample of six-ply set at 10 e.p.i., finished with Philippine edge

Six-ply rug yarn, or its equivalent in two-ply, may be set at approximately twelve e.p.i. to give a close, hardwearing rug; other yarn according to thickness—e.g. a mohair belting yarn may need sixteen multiple e.p.i.

In a warp-face rug, all the pattern is in the warp, and cannot be changed once it is on the loom. It is essential that the pattern is first worked out on paper, for if the exact number of threads to a colour sequence is incorrect the pattern will be badly affected. Very similar patterns to that of a weft-face weave are produced when the weft-face pattern is turned at right angles, but the relationships of the yarns are different, owing to the thickness of the weft.

Simple vertical stripes are produced by warping alternately two or more threads in contrasting colours, in much the same way as weft-face stripes are woven. The warp is made in the usual way, but every time the colour changes, the warp is joined at either end of the warping board.

Horizontal stripes are produced by warping alternate threads in contrasting colours. The two colours may be warped together as one for convenience, and separated in the threading, but make sure that if there is an odd number in the sequence it is joined on in addition, i.e., if there are ten alternating threads of black and white, but the pattern is to begin and end on a black thread, there will have to be eleven black threads, the group consisting of five pairs warped together, and a single black one.

By combining these stripes simple designs of bars and stripes may be woven (fig. 61).

The weaving of a warp-face rug is a little different from other types. Because of the closeness of the setting and the thickness of the yarn, it is advisable to use a four-shaft rather than a two-shaft loom, as the yarns have more room to pass one another on the shafts. The rug is composed of closely-set warp stripes, but not set quite so closely as to be the equivalent of a beaten down weft. In order to compensate, and to make the rug thicker, the hidden weft is very thick, using as many as three strands of six-ply or nine two-ply strands. This means that the colour of the selvedge must match the weft, for this is the only place where the weft will show. Variations in the thickness of the pattern may be achieved by varying the thickness of the weft (fig. 62). The rug in fig. 112, from which fig. 62 is a detail, is another example. Because of the bulk of the warp, it may be necessary to warp in sections, so that the pegs of the warping frame will not be overloaded. When weaving, the weft should be pulled in tightly enough to prevent the warp spreading, unlike weaving a weft-face weave.

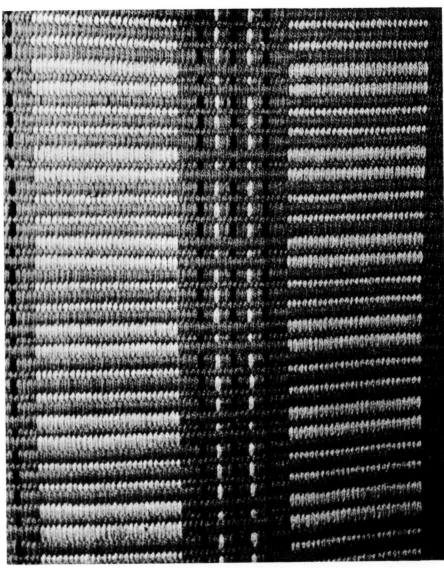

Fig 62   Detail of warp-face rug shown in fig 112. Three strands of two-ply set at 12 e.p.i.

Weaving with unspun fibres

This may be done in several ways. If the unspun fibre is smooth and not very resilient, like hemp or jute, it will lie flat in the weft, and is best combined with other yarns to give variety. The setting will then have to be appropriate to the other yarns, and the warp will show (figs 63, 64). These fibres are long, and are merely woven in bunches of convenient size, splicing roughly to join them.

Fig 63   Matting sample, set at 10 e.p.i. with natural and dyed hemp warp. Raffia, bleached hemp and polished hemp cord weft

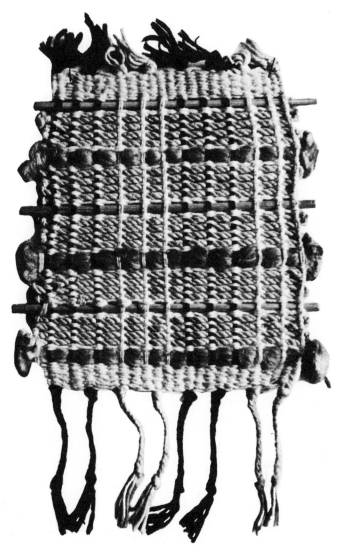

Fig 64   Matting sample, set at 3 e.p.i. in black and white cotton. Split bamboo, polished hemp cord, cotton and unspun jute weft. Ends knotted and plaited

Fleece rugs are exceedingly attractive (fig. 65), and may be woven so that the warp shows, or so that it is completely covered by the fleece. A setting of three or four e.p.i. will achieve either effect, according to the thickness of the fleece. This should be washed and roughly teased apart with the fingers, very slightly twisted, and stuffed into the weft in convenient bundles of, say, about 9 ins long. Each bundle is overlapped slightly, and when

Fig 65   Fleece sample, with linen warp set at 3 e.p.i. Ends knotted and plaited

the whole width is filled, the shed is changed and the weft beaten hard. Attention must be paid to the edges to see that enough fleece is wrapped round. It does not matter if the bundles are not even, as this will adjust itself. As the natural fleece is not the same colour or texture throughout, a pleasing, subtle variation in shade ensues. These rugs wash and wear well as, owing to the characteristics of the wool fibre, the more entangled the fibres become, the more solid the rug. Fleeces of different natural shades may be used, and all unspun fibres may be dyed.

Rag rugs

The rag rug is not merely a way of using up material. It can be very attractive, if attention is paid to the colour and quality of the rags. These should be cut into strips of 1 in. to $1\frac{1}{2}$ ins wide, according to the thickness of the material. They may be cut to within 1 in. of the edge, so that the strip is continuous (fig. 66). The tips of the strip are cut to give a rounded edge, and the join is twisted slightly. Other strips may be tapered and laid together so as to make an even thickness (fig. 67).

Fig 66   Cutting in a continuous strip

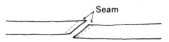

Fig 67   Tapering and joining short strips

The rags should be sorted into colours and types just like any other material, and designing a rag rug is the same as any other sort of designing. The setting should be eight to ten e.p.i. and, as the warp will show, this should be of any suitable strong yarn, which can be dyed to blend in, or make a contrasting feature.

Tapestry techniques

A tapestry woven rug is also a plain-weave rug, but of a special type. Instead of the weft being carried from edge to edge, it is carried backwards and forwards across sections of warp, creating separate blocks of colour. Each change of colour requires a separate weft. The main techniques are:

Khelim

Derived from the Arabic, the word indicates a slit tapestry. The detail from an early nineteenth-century Kurdish Khelim rug (fig. 70) shows this structure, especially where the threads have worn away. The steps are built up at different heights (fig. 68) in order to create the illusion of curves, though basically this is a geometric design.

Built-up shapes

This is only one step removed from Khelim, the shape being built up in smaller steps, each overlapping the other (fig. 69). The cover shows a rug which combines these techniques.

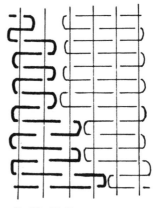

Fig 68   Khelim

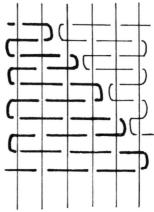

Fig 69   Built-up steps

Fig 70   Detail of nineteenth-century Kurdish Khelim rug. Goat hair and wool mixture warp, wool weft dyed with vegetable dyes

Interlocking round the warp

The weft turns round the same warp end (fig. 71). This has disadvantages, as a ridge may be built up on a vertical slit. It may be combined with slit joins to avoid this ridge, i.e., only interlocking at intervals.

Interlocking weft

The two wefts interlock between the warp ends. The interlock must lie snugly between the warp ends, and the tension of the weft must be adjusted until it is neither pulling nor lying too loosely (fig. 72).

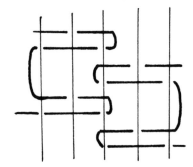

Fig 71   Interlocking round warp

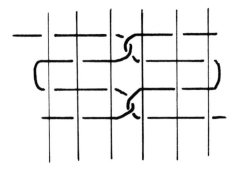

Fig 72   Interlocking between the warp

Outlining a shape

Curves may be built up, leaving a space within the curve. Both sides of the curve have to be built up separately, and care must be taken with the beating, so that both sides are beaten evenly (fig. 73).

After the shape has been built up, a plain weave shed is opened, and the lining weft inserted. This is woven backwards and forwards until enough has been woven, beating down well (fig. 74). The inside of the curve is then built up, the lining again woven round it, and finally the background is completed as before.

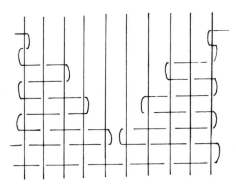

Fig 73   Built-up curve

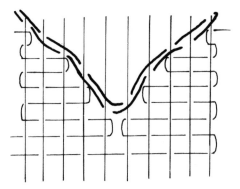

Fig 74   Inserting the lining weft

Fig 75   Rug sample in free tapestry. Cotton warp set at 4 e.p.i. Weft of two strands of two-ply, finished with Damascus edge

Free tapestry

This is a quicker method of producing a shape, but is not so flexible as the conventional tapestry weave (fig. 75). For two colours, a ball of yarn and a shuttle of a different colour is used, winding two yarns together. The shed is opened, and the shuttle woven right through. The yarn on the shuttle is caught through the yarn from the ball, which is kept at one side of the loom, and the doubled yarn is drawn back through the shed to where it is required (fig. 76). The shuttle always goes right through the shed and returns to its own side; the ball always releases a loop which goes to where the colour is required. Three colours may be used, by keeping the shuttle moving in the centre of the shed, two balls of yarn being fed from both sides.

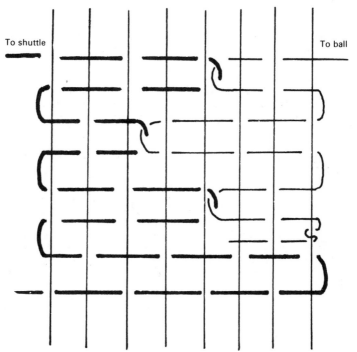

To shuttle

To ball

Fig 76   Free tapestry

Knots and surface techniques

All surface techniques produce a rug which is not reversible, as are most rugs woven in a flat weave. Some techniques, like soumak (p. 72), chaining (p. 75) and partial knotting (p. 48) add only to the appearance, while a knotted pile adds considerably to the warmth and weight. Any surface technique will need one or two rows of plain weave in between, so as to secure the decoration and to make a background.

Knots

The purpose of a knot is to make the pile spring out of the woven background rather than lie flat across it, and the knots used in pile weaving are designed for this purpose. There are three basic types of knot, which have many variations. They may all be used with multiple strands of yarn, and as many of these as may be required should be rolled into balls, and placed in separate containers. The knotting is done on a closed shed.

THE GHIORDES KNOT

This is the most used, and is very secure. It is easier and quicker to knot it from a continuous length than to cut the yarn beforehand. Two warps are raised with the left hand, and the yarn inserted

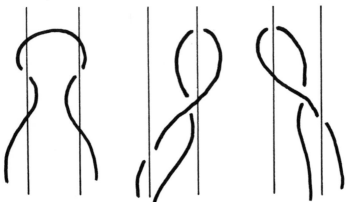

Fig 77   Ghiordes knot
Fig 78   Left-hand Sehna knot
Fig 79   Right-hand Sehna knot

into the centre of these ends. This passes under the right hand warp to the right, then over both warps, to emerge again in the centre (fig. 77). The length of the tuft may then be adjusted and pulled tight before cutting.

THE SEHNA KNOT
Again using a continuous thread, the yarn passes between two warp ends and back to the right, but instead of then passing over the two ends, it goes down through the centre, and under the left warp end. When cut, this knot will lie to the left (fig. 78). It may also be tied the opposite way round, to lie to the right (fig. 79). This is somewhat less secure than the Ghiordes knot, but gives a slightly inclined pile. The second knot may start in the centre of the first (fig. 80), and this will give twice the thickness of pile.

THE SINGLE-WARP KNOT
This is not really a knot, as the yarn simply encircles a single warp end once (fig. 81). It is not as secure as the other two knots, but gives two pile yarns on each warp end, the weft between the rows being beaten down very thoroughly.

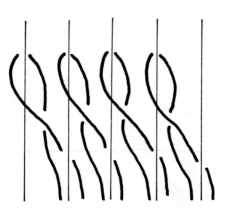

Fig 80   Double Sehna knot

Fig 81   Single-warp knot

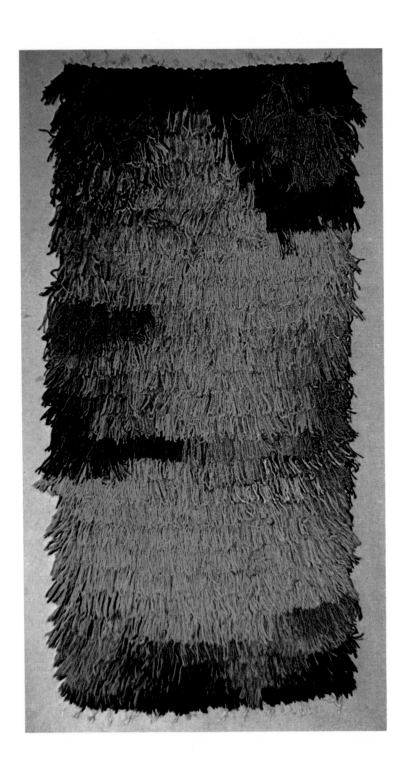

opposite
Fig 82   A rya rug in shades of blue, green and purple dyed by student. Cotton warp set at 5 e.p.i., with 2 $\frac{1}{2}$-in. Ghiordes knotted pile at 2-in. intervals, using three strands of two-ply

Fig 83   Rya rug sample, on cotton warp set at 6 e.p.i. Ground weft in single two-ply, 1 $\frac{1}{2}$-in. pile weft every inch with three strands and occasional dyed linen. Damascus finish, one end has multiple divided plaits, the other plied. Note the design at ends in short sections of vertical striping

The construction of knotted rugs

There are several types of knotted rug, with pile varying from $1/2$ in. to 5 or 6 ins in length. A short pile rug of about $1/2$-in. length is called by its Swedish name, flossa, while the longer pile or rya rugs (figs 82, 83) have a pile length of $1\ 1/2$ ins or more, with a variable area of definition in between.

The number of picks of weft in between determine the appearance of the rug: the more closely the amount of ground weft corresponds to the length of pile, the flatter the pile will lie. A very short pile with one or two weft picks between each row of knots will be almost vertical, while a $2\ 1/2$-in. pile with 2 ins of ground weft will lie fairly flat. A short pile will need to be evenly trimmed, while a long pile may either be cut to lie in a straight line or each knot may vary slightly. The trimming is done every few rows while the weaving progresses, the rug being banged to make the pile stand up while any long ends are trimmed. The pile is best made of wool, but this may be mixed with other fibres such as cotton, linen, jute, mohair or nylon for effect, or these may be used alone.

The setting of the warp may vary between three and ten e.p.i. The closer the setting, the finer the weave and the closer the knots. A setting of three e.p.i. will give a ground weave equivalent to a normal flat woven rug, and the knots will have to be correspondingly thick. I have seen an Italian rug using this setting with a weft of six-ply yarn, the knots being three strands of the same six-ply wool in rows of about 2 ins apart. The result was enormously thick, heavy and luxurious.

In practice a warp set at four or five e.p.i., with a ground weft of one or two strands of two-ply carpet yarn to cover the warp, will give a luxurious appearance combined with economy of materials and speed of weaving. The pile in this instance should be composed of two or three strands of the two-ply yarn.

The selvedge will need special treatment, as the knots never reach entirely to the edge, and the build-up of knots must be compensated for by an extra weft woven in at the edge (fig. 84).

It is almost impossible to estimate quantities of yarn for this type of rug, as this will depend on the length and closeness of the pile, and the distance between the rows of knots. It is best to weave a sample, and calculate approximately from this, remembering that it is better to overestimate than underestimate. This, too, is one of the instances when an unevenly dyed yarn will give lively results, as the combination of the moving tufts and a variety of shades gives a sparkling appearance.

Looping

PULLED-UP LOOPS
This is a process similar to knotting, and also done with a continuous yarn. The simplest way is to pull up loops as needed once a pick has been woven, being careful not to pull them from the shuttle end of the yarn (fig. 85).

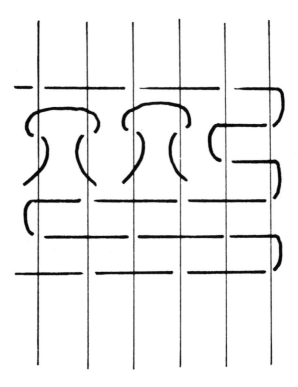

Fig 84   Extra weft at edge

USING A STICK

A stick may be inserted through the loops to keep their size even. If this is done, do not withdraw the stick before the row of plain weave is beaten down. Loops may also be made from any of the knots described, using a stick, or a gauge made from a flat piece of wood. Fig. 86 shows loops being made on a gauge with the Ghiordes knot. The gauge is sometimes grooved on one side and used for cutting the loops to make rya tufts, but the individually cut loop gives a less evenly cut pile, which is more attractive. Loops may also be used with warp-face techniques (fig. 87).

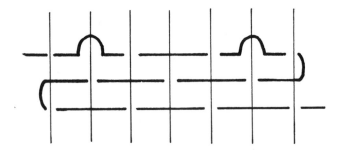

Fig 85   Pulled-up loops

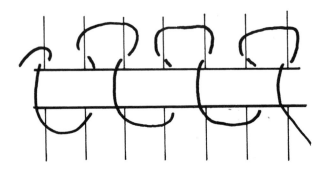

Fig 86   Loops made on a gauge

Fig 87   Pulled-up loops on a warp-face rug sample. Warp of three strands of two-ply set at 10 e.p.i., finished with Philippine edge

Soumak

The word comes from Soumaki, near Shemakha in Transcaucasia, where it was thought to have originated. It is almost an embroidery technique, done on the closed shed. It may be worked all over the rug, giving it a knitted appearance; in bands; or as a motif combined with a flat weave, the soumak weft being carried over two, and back under one warp end (fig. 88). It may also be worked diagonally (fig. 90) and vertically (in the latter form the yarn is simply wound round a single warp end). All forms of soumak, whether as an all-over design or as a linear or block surface decoration, should have one or two rows of ground weave between each row of soumak, and a compensating weft, as in knotting, to prevent the design distorting the ground weave. Soumak may be worked with yarns which are different from the ground, or with the same yarns. The latter produces a textured design which stands out from the ground.

The soumak must be pulled in tightly enough to be firm, but not so tightly that it distorts the warp. On the other hand, if it is too loose, it will not wear well, and tend to catch and pull. A balance must be found between these two extremes. Similarly, the amount of yarn used for soumak will vary according to the effect required. The sampler in fig. 89 shows a variety of uses in yarns of varying thickness. The lower cross is composed of six strands of thinnish mohair, which is not raised very much above the surface. The central motif is composed of six strands of 2-ply carpet yarn, which makes a sharply raised design. The ground weft has no compensating weft (see p. 68, fig. 84), and the resulting distortion may be seen quite clearly.

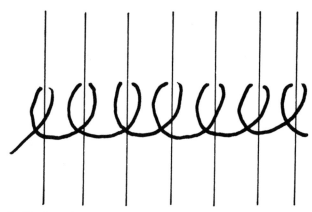

Fig 88   Soumak

Fig 89   Sampler worked with Soumak in various ways

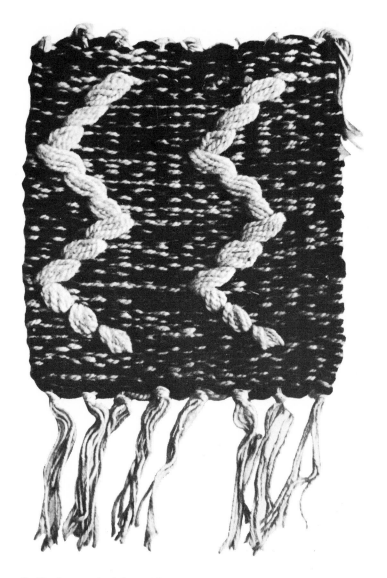

Fig 90   Rug sample of diagonal Soumak on speckled ground. Cotton warp set at 5 e.p.i., weft in two dark, one light two-ply

Chaining

This has a similar appearance to soumak, but is worked with the free end *underneath* the warp. First anchor the chaining yarn by weaving the end into the shed, dropping the rest under the warp. Close the shed, and pull up the yarn through two warp ends, forming a loop. Pull up another loop with the fingers through the next two ends, drawing this through the first loop, and continue in this way across the warp until the end of the section is reached (fig. 91). Weave the chaining yarn back into the shed, locking it into the last loop. Each loop should be tightened as it is worked, as this will make the previous loop firm. Chaining may be worked in any direction as a linear design, or in blocks. There should be three rows of ground weft between each line of chain, and the rules about compensating weft (p. 68, fig. 84) apply here, too (fig. 92).

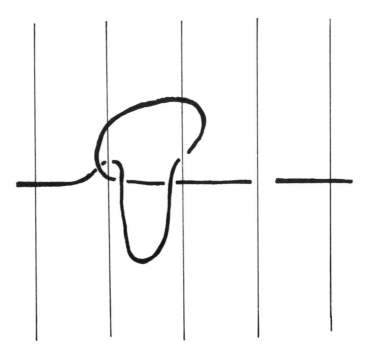

Fig 91   Starting to chain

Fig 92   Sampler of inlay with bands of Soumak and chain

Inlay

An inlaid design, as its name implies, does not physically affect the surface of the rug, which remains flat. Yarns of a different colour from the ground are woven into the same shed as the ground weft, and may be inlaid one row at a time to produce verticals (fig. 93), two rows producing horizontal lines. Fig. 92 shows two similar inlaid motifs, separated by rows of chain and soumak. The inlaid weft is fine mohair, but even so the place where the yarn jumps up between rows shows clearly at the outer edges of the motif. In the upper motif this has been hidden by the tufting round the edge. The jump-up, however, could be used as part of the design. Once again, a compensatory weft (p. 68, fig. 84) should be used to prevent distortion.

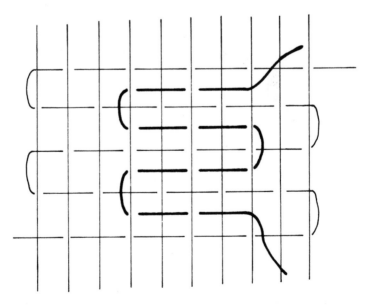

Fig 93   Inlay

Free shuttle

This is similar to inlay in that it uses an extra weft, but instead of being woven in with the ground weave, it acts independently. A pick of plain weave is woven, and the shuttle carrying the extra weft is woven in and out of the closed shed where the pattern weft is wanted (fig. 94). Completely free designs are evolved in this way, the effect being similar to an overshot weave, but not being controlled by the shafts. Care, however, must be taken that the extra weft does not float over too many warp ends, or it will catch and pull. The upper part of fig. 95 shows a free shuttle design.

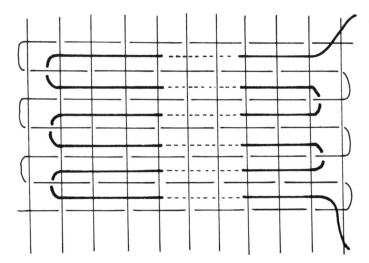

Fig 94   Free shuttle

Fleece

A raised surface may be obtained very simply by weaving in bands of unspun fleece between the rows of ground weft (fig. 95). This may be in rows, or as a motif. There are no rules as to the thickness of the fleece, which should be teased and twisted very slightly to hold it together. The fleece may be natural or dyed.

Fig 95   Sampler with free shuttle design and unspun fleece

The use of drafts

All the techniques so far described may be used on simple frames as well as a loom. There are many techniques which require a four-shaft loom, and for these it is necessary to follow written drafts. It is not within the scope of this book to look at these in detail, but it is essential to know how to read a draft.

Drafting is done on squared (graph) paper, usually with eight squares to the inch. Each row of squares running horizontally corresponds to a shaft on the loom, numbered from front to back. Each vertical row of squares indicates one warp, each threaded in sequence through the healds. This sequence determines the pattern. A straight draft (fig. 96) is threaded in a 1, 2, 3, 4 sequence, which enables a plain weave and a variety of twills to be woven from it. A lifting plan is shown for plain weave, in which alternate shafts are lifted, two at a time, and for a 2 × 2 twill, in which two adjacent shafts are lifted in sequence, moving in one direction one warp at a time. Once these have been mastered, any written draft may be followed. The black squares indicate warps to be lifted, so that the weft passes over the white squares. The white squares, therefore, indicate the surface, the black squares, or warp, being covered by the weft. Because of this, the draft cannot show the whole appearance of the rug, but merely indicates how to weave it.

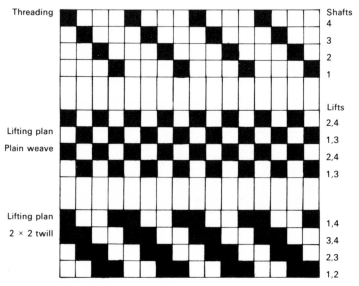

Fig 96   Plain weave and twill

Re-arranged plain weave

A plain weave may be slightly re-arranged to give a different width of stripe. The sample (fig. 98) was woven in alternating colours from the draft (fig. 97) for two shafts, giving blocks of differing widths of stripe. The horizontal bands are woven in picks of three dark, one light, three dark, alternating with light against dark.

Threading

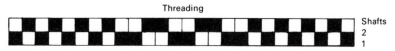

Shafts
2
1

Fig 97   Re-arranged plain weave. The draft is woven in plain weave by lifting alternate shafts

Fig 98   Rug sample, in re-arranged plain weave on two shafts. Cotton warp set at 4 e.p.i., weft in three strands of two-ply

M's and O's

This is a four-shaft extension of the previous weave, in which the blocks are reversed to change the position of the stripes (fig. 99 and frontispiece). The weave is related to the threading. Block A is threaded 1, 2, 3, 4 and if woven 1, 2. 3, 4, lifting adjacent warps, a thick stripe results. If woven 1, 3. 2, 4 the thin stripes appear. Block B is threaded 1, 3. 2, 4, and thick stripes appear when woven as threaded, thin stripes when 1, 2. 3, 4 is lifted. Because the thick stripe is looser, the weft is distorted. If each section is only woven for a short time, a textured pattern appears, with no distortion (fig. 100).

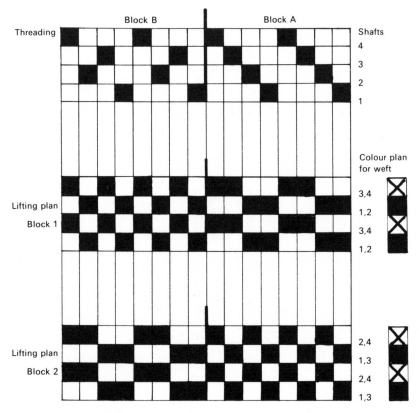

Fig 99   M's and O's

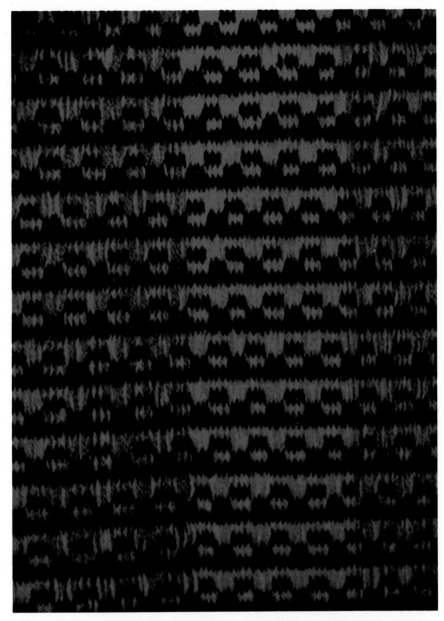

Fig 100   M's and O's rug detail, in black and shades of red. This has a three-dimensional effect, similar to the rug in the frontispiece but without the distortion, due to the small size of the blocks

Bound weaving on opposites

In order to cover the warp, each time a pick is woven on one pair of shafts, a contrasting pick is woven on the other pair. A 2 × 2 twill draft woven in this way is shown in fig. 101.

Rosepath

A favourite weave, on which many variations are possible (fig. 102). It may be woven as a normal rosepath with a plain weave binding thread between each row of pattern, producing a textured surface (figs 102A and 103). A heavier, flat-surfaced rug may be woven in bound opposites, with no plain weave binder (figs 102B and 104). The setting is approximately 8 e.p.i, woven with three strands of 2-ply for the pattern weft, one strand for the binder when this is used.

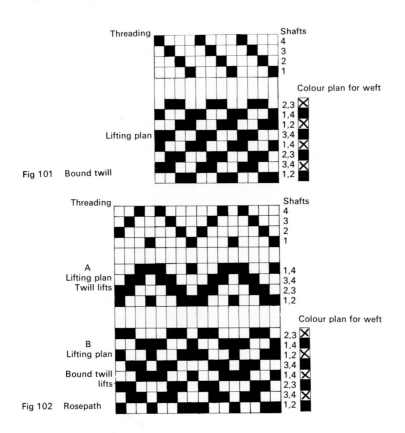

Fig 101   Bound twill

Fig 102   Rosepath

Fig 103   Rosepath rug sample, with plain weave binder

Fig 104   Rosepath rug sample, in bound weave

Honeycomb

This is difficult to understand from the draft, but easy on the loom (fig. 105). The ground is woven in one strand of two-ply, the heavy honeycomb pick in six or eight strands. The ground is woven in blocks on the two front shafts alternating with the two back shafts, each block beating down and distorting the thick pattern weft woven in the plain weave shed (fig. 106). The blocks may be threaded in any width, and woven in varying lengths, care being taken to end and begin with the opposite shed to the plain weave shed. The setting is six to eight e.p.i.

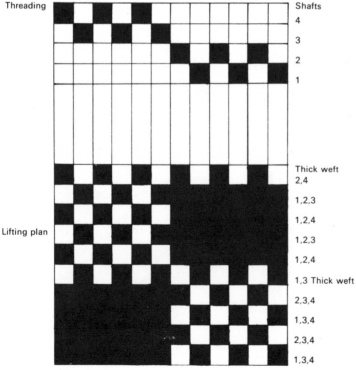

Fig 105   Honeycomb

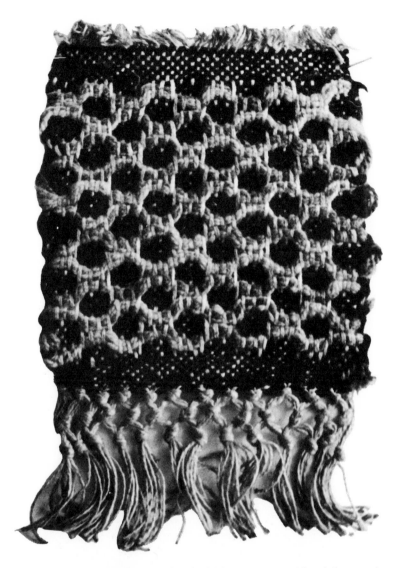

Fig 106   Rug sample, in honeycomb with hemp warp set at 10 e.p.i. Honeycomb weft in eight strands of two-ply, ground in single two-ply

Summer and winter

Another favourite textured weave on two blocks (fig. 107), the pattern reversing on the other side of the rug. Threaded at five e.p.i. with four strands of two-ply, the plain weave binder is a single strand. There are a number of variations on this weave (fig. 108). Note that the plain weave is obtained on shafts 1, 2. 3, 4, and the pattern lifts are related to the threading.

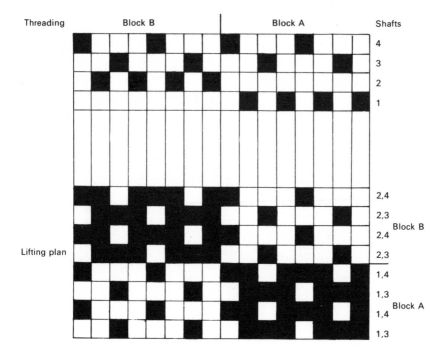

Fig 107   Summer and winter

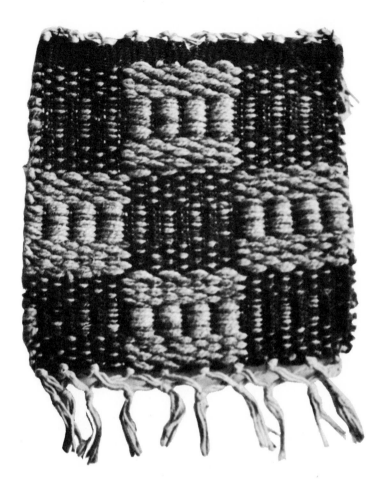

Fig 108   Rug sample, in Summer and winter on cotton warp set at 5 e.p.i. Fringed
with divided knots

Double weave

The pattern is picked up by hand in this weave (fig. 109), which makes a light rug (fig. 110). Using two-ply carpet yarn for both warp and weft, threaded at sixteen e.p.i. in alternate colours, the weft is woven in these alternate colours, raising shafts 1 and 3 for one colour and lowering shafts 2 and 4 for the other. This makes two plain-weave faces which are interchangeable. The pattern is made by bringing the back face through to the front where the pattern is needed. Again, this is more easily understood on the loom.

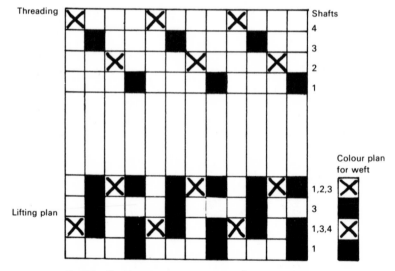

Fig 109   Double weave

Fig 110   Rug sample, in double weave using a four-ply worsted equivalent to two-ply carpet yarn for both warp and weft

Other methods

In addition to the techniques described, there are several other ways of making rugs, some with woven techniques, some in an entirely different manner.

Inkle strips

An inkle loom (fig. 111) is a device for weaving narrow braids. The entire length of the warp is wound on to the frame, alternate threads passing through a loop and across the frame, regulating the raising and lowering of the shed. These threads, usually about forty-eight, are woven so that they lie closely together, hiding the weft completely, and giving a width of between two or three inches according to the thickness of the warp. This gives a warp-face weave of the same type as woven on a full width, illustrated in fig. 112. The finished strips are joined together to make a rug.

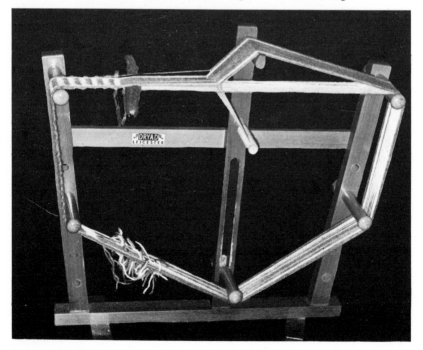

Fig 111   Inkle loom

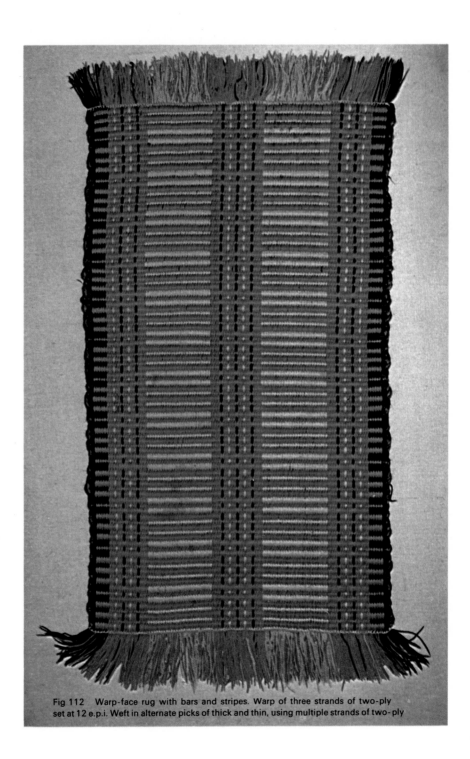

Fig 112   Warp-face rug with bars and stripes. Warp of three strands of two-ply set at 12 e.p.i. Weft in alternate picks of thick and thin, using multiple strands of two-ply

Tablet strips

Again, this is a rug in the form of woven strips, the weaving achieved by means of a number of tablets, or square cards with holes punched in each corner. Individual threads are passed through each hole and, when stretched, these threads form the warp, the movement of which is controlled by turning the tablets (fig. 113). A firm strip is woven, the warp being twisted and held in place by the weft.

Both tablet and inkle strips are sewn together with a figure-of-eight, making sure that the tension of each strip is kept even.

Hooked rugs

These may be made with coarse canvas as a backing, about sixteen threads to the inch each way. The pile is inserted with either a latched hook or a punch needle, the length of the pile being adjustable. The design is first drawn on the canvas, which may then be held loose on the lap or stretched on a frame, the latter being preferable. With the hook method, a loop is pulled up through the spaces between the backing threads (fig. 114) every one or two spaces, according to the thickness of the yarn and the density required. The punch needle, on the other hand, pushes the yarn between the spaces (fig. 115) working from the back of the canvas. The loops so formed may be cut or uncut, and the medium allows the loops to be worked in any direction, taking care to adjust the height of the pile evenly. The Tibetan design shown in fig. 116 was adapted for the hooked rug in fig. 117. Note the **way in** which the design has been simplified for this purpose.

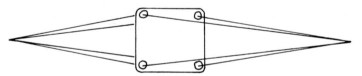

Fig 113   Four ends of warp passed through holes in tablet

Fig 114   Pulled loops

Fig 115   Pushed loops

Fig 116   Design traced from
a Tibetan painting for rug in
fig 117

Fig 117   A hooked rug, using three strands of two-ply in a punch needle. Note
how the details of the design have been simplified. The pictorial rugs of this weaver
were inspired by themes encountered in her work as a curator at Liverpool Museums

Braiding

Braided rugs are a non-woven variation of the rag rug. Three or more strips of rag are plaited together in a flat plait, the ends of the strips being joined to make a continuous length. The joins should not occur at the same place in the plait. The plaits, or braids, are then coiled and sewn together to make round or oval shapes (fig. 118). Other materials, such as rug yarn, yarn oddments, and rush may also be plaited and sewn to make this sort of rug.

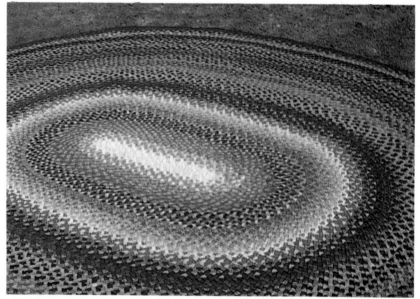

Fig 118   Braided rug

Wrapped cord

Two cords are wrapped together by a figure-of-eight binding
(fig. 119), which may be coloured in order to introduce pattern.
This wrapped strip is coiled and sewn together, wrapping and
sewing every few inches to keep the rug flat. The cords may be
heavy cotton, or yarn oddments, the wrapping being rug yarn or
any other suitable pliable yarn.

Clip rugs

These are our grandmothers' pile rugs made of rags, and may have
either a woven background or a canvas backing. Rag is cut in the
same way as for woven rag rugs, and may be knotted into the
background in the usual way. The same standard of design must
be applied to these rugs, and careful attention should be paid to
this aspect.

Knitting and crochet

Rugs may be made in either of these techniques, in either wool
or rag strips, but will tend to stretch out of shape unless they are
backed. To ensure the maximum firmness, small needles or hooks
should be used in relation to the coarse yarn, which should be
the equivalent of at least a six-ply rug yarn. Fringe, if needed, will
have to be inserted into the ends after the rug is completed.

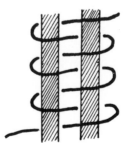

Fig 119   Wrapped cords

Finishes

After a rug is woven, the ends must be finished securely. This protects the ends of the rug, and also provides a decorative finish. The first end may be finished while the rug is still on the loom, slipping it under the back bar, and back towards you so that there is something to pull against. The other end is untied from the back rod and held in place by weights on a table. If this is difficult, place the rug on your knee and wedge it against the underside of the table, so that a section is held securely, making sure that the edge is kept even.

Overhand knot

This is the easiest knot to use. Push a group of ends hard up against the weaving, and tie the knot (fig. 120). Then divide it into two and pull it apart, thus tightening it against the weaving. Tie the knots evenly, at intervals of not more than one inch. More than one knot may be tied in each bunch if desired, the ends being cut evenly about $1/2$ in. beyond the knot. The knots may be subdivided to make further rows of knots.

Plying

Divide the ends into equal groups and ply them together by twisting in the same direction as the twist of the yarn, thus increasing the tightness of the twist. Then twist the two plies in the opposite direction, and finish off with a knot (fig. 121). Do not twist too much, or the end will not lie flat.

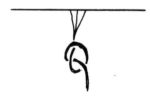

Fig 120 Overhand knot

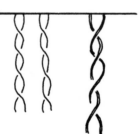

Fig 121 Plying

Plaiting

Either a three strand or a multiple plait (braid) may be used, the ends being finished by knotting or whipping, cutting them $1/2$ in. beyond the knot (fig. 122).

Sennits

These are cords made from half-knots. Three units of ends are used, one of which is a central core (fig. 123). Place the left-hand end over the centre, holding them together, then bring the right-hand end through both the other ends and up through the loop. Holding the centre end, pull the other two tight. This will make a spiral effect if repeated. Tying the knot in the opposite direction will make the spiral turn the other way, and if the knot is tied in both directions alternately the finish will lie flat. This is one of the macramé techniques, any of which may be used for finishing. Such an edge is shown in fig. 124, the ends being plaited and whipped.

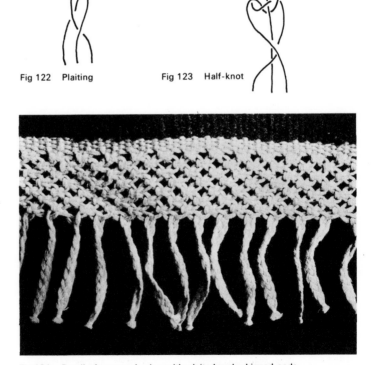

Fig 122   Plaiting   Fig 123   Half-knot

Fig 124   Detail of macramé edge with plaited and whipped ends

Philippine edge

This is one of a series of continuous knots forming a ridge which protects the weft. It works on a unit of three ends, the right-hand end being taken over and behind the other two, emerging between the second and third end (fig. 125). The first end is now discarded and the fourth end ties the knot, after which the second end is discarded. A ridge is formed by the knots and, if the rug is turned over, a second ridge may be made.

Damascus edge

This is a similar edge, working on a two-end unit. The right-hand end is taken left, over and round the second end, and pulled away from you (fig. 126). The second end is then knotted round the third, and so on. The ends are now lying on the body of the rug. In the same way as before, knot the first right-hand end round the second, but this time pull towards you (fig. 127).

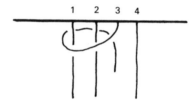

Fig 125   Philippine edge

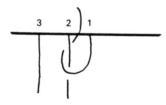

Fig 126   Damascus edge, stage 1

Fig 127   Damascus edge, stage 2

History

The earliest coverings for floors were hay, bracken, rushes, etc., which were strewn on the floor and renewed periodically. Later, rushes were plaited or woven into mats.

Knotted carpets originated in the East in ancient times, and were used first on the walls and floors of tents. Both Khelims and knotted rugs were used for this purpose, later for prayer rugs and bed coverings.

From Turkey the use of rugs spread into Europe via Greece and Rome, and later through the Moorish invasion of Spain. Some of these Spanish rugs were brought to England in the thirteenth century when Eleanor of Castile married Edward I. Later, Cardinal Wolsey received sixty rugs as a present from Venice, and from then on rugs were substantially used as a floor covering. The first English rug was made in 1570, only ten in existence being made before 1600. Rugs may be seen in many paintings of noble houses —from Souch's painting of Sir Thomas Aston at the death-bed of his wife (in Manchester City Art Gallery), where plaited rush may be seen on the floor, to the sumptuous Holbein portrait of Henry VIII in the Walker Art Gallery, Liverpool, which shows a rug.

The Revocation of the Edict of Nantes in 1685 brought weavers from France. They settled in Kidderminster, Wilton and Axminster, which were already centres for carpet making, and continue to be to this day.

Up to Victorian times, increasing industrialization reduced the use of hand-knotting, though some has still been done at the Royal Wilton factory until very recently. William Morris revived the art of hand-knotting, and through him, and people like Aristide Messinisi, the rise of the modern artist-weaver was made possible. Peter Collingwood, with Tadek Beutlich, Gwen and Barbara Mullins and Ronald Grierson are the chief exponents of the craft in England, and have been responsible for teaching many of the growing number of people practising rug weaving today.

List of suppliers

Rug yarn

Charles Butterworth, 2222 East Susquehanna Avenue, Philadelphia 25, Pennsylvania.

Contessa Yarns, Department HW, PO Box 37, Lebanon, Connecticut 16279.

Craft Yarns of Rhode Island Inc., 603 Mineral Springs Avenue, Pawtucket, Rhode Island 02860.

Creative Handweavers, 3827 Sunset Boulevard, Los Angeles, California.

The Mannings, East Berlin, Pennsylvania 13716.

Paternayan Bros, 312 East 9th Street, New York, N. Y. 10028.

Looms and equipment

Gilmore Looms, 1032 North Broadway Avenue, Stockton, California 95205.

Leclerc Looms, 312 East 23rd Street, New York, N. Y. 10010.

Structo Artcraft, King-Seeley Thermos Co., Freeport, Illinois.

Rug and linen warp yarn

Lily Mills Co., Department HWH, Shelby, North Carolina.

Marine cords and twines

Mrs. Lyle B. Robinson, 1019 N. E. 62nd Street, Seattle, Washington 98115.

Rug yarn and equipment

Craftool Co., 1 Industrial Rd., Woodridge, N. J. 07075.

The Yarn Depot, 545 Sutter Street, San Francisco, California 94102.

For further reading

Byways in handweaving by Mary Meigs Atwater; Collier-Macmillan, London 1954 (detailed instructions for tablet and inkle designs)

Create with yarn by Ethel Jane Beitler; International Textbook Co., Scranton, Penn., 1964 (a section on hooked rugs)

Introducing macramé by Eiran Short; Batsford, London 1970; Watson-Guptill, New York 1970

Notes on carpet knotting and weaving by C. E. C. Tattersall; Victoria and Albert Museum, London 1961; 2nd ed 1969

Rug-making by Mary Allard; Pitman, London 1963; Chilton, Philadelphia 1963

Rugweaving by Klares Lewes and Helen Hutton; Batsford, London 1962; Branford, Newton Center, Mass 1962

Rugweaving for everyone by Gallinger and Del Deo; Bruce Publishing Co., New York, 1957

Simple weaving by Hilary Chetwynd; Studio Vista, London 1969; Watson-Guptill, New York 1969

The Ashley book of knots by Clifford Ashley; Faber, London 1941; Doubleday, New York 1944 (a comprehensive guide to knotting for a variety of uses)

The techniques of rug weaving by Peter Collingwood; Faber, London 1968; Watson-Guptill, New York 1968 (an essential book for the seriously interested student)

The technique of weaving by John Tovey; Batsford, London 1965; Reinhold, New York 1966

Vegetable dyeing by Alma Lesch; Watson-Guptill, New York 1970

Woven rugs by Ronald Grierson; Dryad Press, London 1952; 2nd ed 1960

Yarn dying by Elsie Davenport; Sylvan Press 1955; Craft and Hobby Book Service, Pacific Grove, California 1970

Your handweaving by Elsie Davenport; Sylvan Press 1951; Craft and Hobby Book Service, Pacific Grove, California 1970

Index

Set in 9 point Univers
Printed and bound by Parish Press, Inc.